50 WAYS TO EAT COCK

HEALTHY CHICKEN RECIPES WITH BALLS!

ADRIENNE HEW, CN
"THE NUTRITION HERETIC"

DISCLAIMER

The content of this book is provided as information only and may not be construed as medical or health advice. No action or inaction should be taken solely on the basis of the information provided here. Please consult with a licensed health professional or doctor on any matter relating to your health and wellbeing.

The information and opinions expressed in this book are believed to be accurate and factual based upon the resources available to the authors at the time of writing. Readers who fail to consult with the appropriate health authorities assume the risk of any and all injuries.

The publisher is not responsible for errors or omissions.

BOOKS IN THE HEALTH ALTERNATIPS SERIES

Drowning in 8 Glasses: 7 Myths about Water Revealed

*Frenching Your Food: 7 Guilt-Free French Diet Tips to Slim Down,
Look Younger and Live Longer without Calorie Counting or Strenuous Exercise*

BOOKS IN THE AFFORDABLE ORGANICS AND GMO-FREE SERIES

50 Ways to Eat Cock: Healthy Chicken Recipes with Balls!

Honeylingus: 50 Healthy Honey Recipes that Will Leave You Begging for More!

*Good Times, Great Food: Fighting Childhood Obesity and Picky Eating One
Celebration at a Time (coming soon)*

SPECIAL GIFTS FOR YOU!

Want a sneak peek at some outrageously delicious recipes from my new book, *Honeylingus: 50 Healthy Honey Recipes that Will Leave You Begging for More*? Looking for more information on what's safe and healthy to eat? Want *real* answers to your health questions?

Grab all these and more by going to http://honeyling.us to claim your FREE gifts today!

TABLE OF CONTENTS

INTRODUCTION

CHOKING THE CHICKEN

It was a beautiful, sunny Sunday morning in September when I started out for the highway. Before leaving the house, I had nervously entered the destination's address into the GPS, but in my anxious state, had little faith that it would send me to the right place. Throughout the entire half hour drive, I wondered to myself if I were able to carry out the task ahead of me.

Earlier that week, my friend, Michelle, who owns the local health food store had invited me to her farm for that day to help her and her husband complete an unusual Sunday afternoon ritual – the slaughter of 50 cocks (also known as roosters).

Normally Michelle and her husband, René, had raised hens (female chickens), but in that particular year, the hatchery sent them all male chicks. The salesman at the hatchery assured them that these birds would be fine eating when grown to full size, but what they found was quite different and not at all pleasurable to the modern palate. The birds were tough and straw-like, dry and difficult to chew.

Knowing not only my penchant for trying new recipes, but also my interest in pursuing a challenge, Michelle figured that I would be the perfect candidate for finishing the job they had started the Sunday before. In fact, she was so disheartened by the results of some of the recipes she had tried, that she offered to pay me in cocks – 25 to be exact – knowing that I would jump at the chance

3

to play around with them.

As a holistic nutritionist, who must to remain pragmatic in all things pertaining to food, that September morning was to be the ultimate test of my pragmatism. Many people's food choices are based upon ideology and perceptions of cruelty towards animals. However, in my business, such a stance can be quite literally fatal, should someone deny him or herself a piece of meat that might be crucial to reversing a disease. Yet eating a piece of meat and killing an animal are two very different events for most people in industrialized societies. I was no different from any other city slicker and on the drive to my friend's house, I worried that I was perhaps too chicken to step up to the plate and lop their heads off.

When I stepped out of the car, the air was clean and crisp. To the innocent bystander, it would not have been apparent that in a few moments time, the scene would become far more sobering.

I walked up the stone steps into the house, where I was warmly welcomed. Michelle and I sat around chatting for a few minutes, giggling and gossiping about the absurdity of the week's newsworthy events. A few moments later, René showed up in the truck with our victims.

One-by-one, the birds were let out of the cage, knowing that their life's purpose was about to be fulfilled. It was amazing to me how calm they were. Many farmers had told me before that animals ready for slaughter "understood the deal" and willingly submitted to their fate. Seeing this play out gave me a new understanding of the cycle of life as well as terms like "food chain". This also gave me an even deeper appreciation for honoring any food that ends up on my plate, whether animal or vegetable.

Immediately after slaughter, a pot of very hot water was kept nearby for the purpose of de-feathering the bodies. Then the birds were all brought inside the house for the tedious task of removing the entrails and feet. The bodies were then bagged individually; heads and feet bagged separately for making rich nutritious stock;

and gizzards, livers and hearts sorted and stored in their respective packages.

Many hours later, I returned to my car with 25 cocks in a cooler to stuff in the trunk. This is where the real challenge began – finding delicious ways of preparing these tough old birds.

HOW TO STROKE YOUR COCK

As I drove home, I began to think of the many ways I could prepare my first cock when I got home. I knew that the tough, dry nature of the meat meant that would not lend itself to quick cooking such as frying, sautéing or even baking. Whatever the preparation, it would require long cooking, preferably in a moist, liquid base. Some experts claim that if the cock is young enough – less than one year old – that it could be cooked just like a young spring chicken. These lean lads were a mere six months old, but based upon Michelle's experience with them, they were way too tough to be enjoyed by any of the faster cooking methods.

The French dish *coq au vin* came to mind first. This dish, which today is more commonly prepared with the female of the species, from its name clearly originated with a rooster in the pot. The same goes for cock-a-leekie, a traditional Scottish soup, which despite its rather humorous name is quite delicious.

Unlike their female counterparts, cocks have a lean, sleek body type instead of a more rounded, voluptuous shape. As a result of this physique, they yield larger amounts of bone-building, stomach-soothing gelatin into every dish in which they appear, and a deep, rich flavor unparalleled by any hen.

One type of cock that does not fit this body type is the capon. Capons, or castrated cocks, are widely recognized as the best of both worlds for their nutritional value and delectable flavor. Since cocks do not lose part of their nutritional intake in the production of eggs, it is thought that they maintain more of the nutrition that they ingest within the body. However, the removal of the testes makes them prone to gaining weight in the same way that a hen would. Therefore the meat is plump, tender and juicy, while maintaining its robust flavor and nutritional profile.

The more I contemplated the variety of ways that these birds could be prepared, the more I realized that cock could very well be lurking in nearly every processed "chicken" product on the market. On traditional farms (and presumably on commercial farms), the females of various animals tend to serve long-term functions in food production such as bearing offspring as well as producing milk and eggs. On the other hand, with the exception of oxen, which once upon a time would have been used to plow fields, male farm animals serve virtually no purpose once they have been used for breeding and therefore are often the first to end up on the dinner plate. The ornery cock is no exception to this rule. Something to think about that the next time you reach for chicken nuggets or canned chicken soup.

As you might imagine, today, it is rather difficult to find 50 recipes specifically calling for a cock as the main ingredient. I consulted many people around the globe about their countries' cock-eating traditions and while nearly everyone had some anecdotal stories or advice to give about eating cock, very few were able to produce recipes requiring it as the main ingredient. Even their grandparents had forgotten the recipes their parents used to prepare for them.

Knowing the basic principles of long, moist-heat cooking I was able to adapt many chicken recipes to cock cookery. In fact, it is entirely possible that many of today's recipes calling for a stewing hen would have used a cock interchangeably a century ago.

Buying a cock, however, may be easier than you think. The first place to look is at a local farm or a farmer's market. Farmers are always looking for ways to get rid of extra cocks, since they tend to fight with one another. Often, they will sell them at a deep discount since most people have no idea how to prepare them.

Another option is to ask in Asian or Caribbean markets. You may have a few language hurdles to overcome in some Asian markets, but know that 'cock' is typically the preferred term in either of these markets. Sometimes the term 'cockerel' is used in Caribbean markets. It is sad to note that real cock or cockerel are rapidly being replaced in Caribbean markets by highly processed packets of MSG-filled cock soup mixes.

If you have searched and searched and still have trouble locating cock, then opt for a stewing hen. Stewing hens are laying chickens that have past their prime for tenderness. Although they are often available in many supermarkets, you may also ask for them at farmer's markets as well, where often they are sold whole for less than half that of a younger, more tender chicken. While many connoisseurs may feel that the flavor is less robust, it still makes a fine substitute in any of these recipes.

If all else fails, feel free to substitute a spring chicken or fryer, if necessary. Note that these chickens require less cooking, so cooking time may be reduced by as much as half.

One cock to steer clear of for purposes of these recipes is capon, which are more suited to roasting and more rapid forms of cooking. Capons are a delicacy and are usually only available during the Christmas holidays. As such, the price is similar to that of a 20 lb. turkey. So my recommendation here is more based upon economics than any inherent grudge against the capon.

COCK OF AGES

Years ago as a college student in Spain, I spent winter vacation in Portugal to visit my Portuguese pen pal. Having forgotten my watch back at home in Madrid, I had to rely on the local cocks to wake me up. At the time, I thought that Portuguese cocks were somehow confused or otherwise had not read the "how to be a good cock" training manual because crowed at all hours of the night, well before the sun made its appearance for the day. In researching this book, I found that roosters everywhere have trouble recognizing the day's first light and crow to claim their turf at any time of day or night.

During my visit I noticed that nearly every Portuguese souvenir bore the symbol of a rooster on it. "What a peculiar national symbol!", I thought to myself. Of course, it was hard for me to resist bringing home a little cock statue that was supposed to change colors when rain was approaching. Just like the alarm-clock cocks that should not have awakened me before the sun came up, it did not work as expected either. I later learned from my Portuguese friend that the rooster is thought to bring good luck, which is why every family has at least a few cocks lurking around their house.

It was only at the writing of this section of the book that a good friend of mine reminded me of the cock's importance to the French people. The French have long had strong ties to the cock for one important reason: the Latin word for cock, *gallus*, is quite similar to the Latin word for inhabitants of Gaul (the Latin word for France), *gallicus*. As such, the cock has gone on to adorn everything from the kings' emblems and flags to coins and stamps. Today, the cock proudly continues to take its place on the logos of many national sports teams.

As it turns out, cocks have played an important role in many cultures. Reverence for this animal stems from two main characteristics: the cock's crow, *cock-a-doodle-doo*, which serves as a reminder of his constant vigilance and his tough-guy personality, which translates to courage and service as a protector.

Even though many modern humans concur that roosters crow whenever they feel like it, ancient man was quite impressed by the cock's ability to distinguish dark from light. For this reason, used the cock's morning crow as an alarm clock. Today, we still can see the animal honored for keeping a watchful eye by its place on weathervanes. There are, however, a few nuances in man's appreciation for the bird.

For the ancient Greeks, the rooster's morning cry was recognized more widely as victory over the darkness of night. As a result, the rooster came to symbolize not only the sun, but its image was used in honor of several gods including Zeus and his son, Apollo, as well as Attis and Persephone. At the same time, lions feared them, so they were also quite respected as an animal of valor.

In contrast, Nordic and Celtic cultures did not associate *cock-a-doodle-doo* with the heavens, but with the Underworld. While the cry still symbolized vigilance, it was accepted as a warning of impending dangers and an ode to soldiers fallen in battle.

In the Bible, it is said that after Peter denied Christ, a cock crowed three times, making it the official symbol of Jesus's suffering. (In some versions of the Bible, Peter denies Jesus three times before the rooster crows twice.) This event is commemorated by placing weathervanes on top of many churches.

While western cultures each seem to have their own historic

relationships to rooster, Asian cultures seem to have maintained the richest culture revolving around the cock. A sacred symbol to the Japanese, these little guys continue to run free in Shinto temples where they serve to call worshipers to early morning prayers.

Ask the Chinese about the rooster and you will learn that it is a *yang* creature, referring to its very male attributes of being thin, hot, dry and muscular all of which translate into fidelity, strength, courage and even bossiness. Yet along with all of these macho characteristics, cocks have also come to symbolize honesty, watchfulness, protection and pride.

This precious animal, revered for the treasures found throughout its body have made it an essential ingredient in Traditional Chinese Medicine throughout the centuries. The testicles, for example, rich in testosterone are not only considered beneficial for a man's virility, but help balance hormones in females resulting in a clear complexion. Meanwhile the gizzard, which is used by the rooster to grind its food after swallowing, is prescribed to aid in our own digestion. True to Chinese tradition, these are not the only parts of the animal that are used, but the rest of the bird ends up in the stock pot and its meat used in a variety of dishes.

Due to its lean body mass and testosterone-rich constitution, consuming cock meat and broth is an ideal approach to losing excess weight. Estrogen levels tend to be very high in overweight people. It is after all the hormone that gives women their curves. Testosterone displaces estrogen thereby encouraging the body to gain more muscle and lose fat.

In the practice of *feng shui*, the spatial arrangement of objects in relation to the flow of energy, the cock is closely associated with career advancement. He wakes up early in the morning to get a start on the new day and productivity. Using pictures, statues or other representations of roosters in one's prescribed "*feng shui* directions" will help achieve the desired career goals.

Every 12 years, the Chinese zodiac celebrates the "Year of the Cock". I was fortunate enough to be born under this sign.

Although the cock is regarded as *yang*, in the Chinese zodiac it is associated with the metal element, which is *yin* (cold). Therefore it is considered a *yin* sign within the zodiac. While the rooster may appear to be feisty and flamboyant, it is also trustworthy, hardworking and down-to-earth with a disdain for those who are dishonest, impolite or have a poor sense of hygiene.

In relationships, roosters often take the lead and can be quite demanding of their partners. So it is always ideal for a cock to be paired with someone who can knock them down a few pegs, when they get a bit too caught up in being boastful or arrogant.

As mentioned before, cocks are real go-getters when it comes to matters of business and often are quite successful in their careers by making work a top priority. Roosters may be successful at virtually any business they set their minds to and are equally suited to highly scientific and mathematical fields such as dentistry and accounting as they are to more artistic endeavors such as acting and music.

Asia is not the only place where cocks play an important part in nutrition and health. Since childhood, I recall my mother talking about cockerel (young cock) soup, a traditional Jamaican soup often fed to pregnant women to ensure that her baby would receive the best nutrition possible and be born free of disease. Its sodium-rich broth also helps to keep morning sickness at bay. Americans often chuckle to find cock soup sold in packets at West Indian grocery stores, not recognizing the impact real cock soup has on health. In an age where autism and allergies run rampant amongst our youth, perhaps it is time to revisit this simple plan for building sturdy children from the start.

The cock has certainly influenced our language as well. The bright, colorful feathers of the rooster have given us the term "cocktail" in reference to the blending of different spirits or wines of various colors. Meanwhile, the term "cockpit", which refers to the pilot's compartment on an aircraft, has less glorious origins in a blood sport called "cockfighting".

Cockfighting has existed since ancient times. In the sport, two specially raised cocks are placed in a ring, the cockpit, to fight one another, sometimes to the death. Although increasingly rare, cockfights are still largely performed in many parts of Southeast Asia and even in the West, where it is frowned upon for its brutality.

On a recent trip to Costa Rica, I had the opportunity to tour the private estate of a Cuban businessman, who allowed his brother to dedicate an entire building on his property to raising gamecocks. Luckily, the birds had been permanently removed at the time that I visited, a few years after the brother's untimely death.

Suffice it to say that cocks have been important to humans since the beginning of their relationship. We see them in symbols and hear them in our everyday language. Now it's your turn to re-learn how to use them in your cooking and as a powerful adjunct to your health.

KEEPING IT DELICIOUS, NUTRITIOUS AND CHEAP

You may find the title of this book funny, racy, or even raunchy. The information contained in these pages, however, is written from my perspective as a nutritionist. So if you are interested in dispelling some of the nutritional taboos that plague the way most people eat today, read on. If you just want to get started on eating some cock, feel free to skip ahead to the recipes.

Fifty Ways to Eat Cock is part of my *Affordable Organics and GMO-Free* series of books. Many people shy away from organics and GMO-free foods because of the perceived cost. However, foods like cock show that not only can it be reasonable, it can be downright cheaper than even conventional foods. I have bought pastured, organic cocks and stewing hens for as little as four dollars each. When was the last time you found a deal like that on hormone-pumped, grain-fed battery chicken?

Since the rest of the book focuses on eating cock, this section discusses why the recipes follow certain techniques and normally forbidden ingredients. It is my job as a nutritionist to teach people how to make their diets more digestible and their nutrients more easily assimilated. For many readers, this will be an introduction to cooking traditional foods and a completely new way of thinking about the human diet. For those already familiar with these techniques, it will hopefully serve as an additional resource for cooking delicious traditional foods that appeal to a modern palate.

If you haven't realized by now, I am not your typical whole-foods nutritionist, hence the moniker, *The Nutrition Heretic*. Over the years, I have had many mentors including doctors, nutritionists and researchers. They have helped me understand that eating well can be simple, just by combining a diet of foods from both the plant and animal kingdom. Yet there are several key areas of nutrition where many conventional and holistic health practitioners continue to parrot semi-truths established by the food processing industry. These companies have made billions of dollars by scaring people away from real foods and then selling products that swoop in to save the day. Below are a few examples as they pertain to this book:

FATS

You will notice that many of the recipes in the book call for animal fats that nearly every other health professional in the United States would warn you *against* eating. Animal fats were a significant source of energy until 100 years ago. Contrary to popular belief, people who ate these fats routinely lived longer than people do today. In the book *Diet & Heart Disease*, author Stephen Byrnes notes that a report in the *Journal of American Oil Chemists* showed that "animal fat consumption had declined from 104 grams per person per day in 1909, to 97 grams per day in 1972, while vegetable fat intake had increased from a low 21 grams to almost 60 grams. Total fat consumption had increased, as the proponents of the Lipid Hypothesis argued, but this increase was mostly due to vegetable oils with 50 percent coming from liquid oils and the other 41 percent from margarine made from vegetable oils."

Comparatively, animal fats contain higher amounts of saturated fatty acids than modern vegetable oils. These fatty acids are easily recognized by the body and contribute to the body's healthy absorption of nutrients. The fact that saturated fat is an important nutrient for both the heart and intestines was once common knowledge published in nutrition and medical textbooks. This would conflict with modern nutritional dogma that wants us to believe that natural animal fats, the saturated ones in particular, are the cause of disease. The modern approach would have us believe that our bodies prefer to use fake, rancid oils and fats, such as margarine and canola.

In addition to their importance to the heart and intestines, animal fats are an important source of the fat-soluble vitamins A, D, E and K. They are also important to cellular integrity. Without saturated fats to lubricate the joints, mucous membranes and skin, joint disease, asthma and skin eruptions become common problems. Along with cholesterol, these fats regulate our hormones, prevent mood swings and slow the uptake of sugar in the blood.

Popular reports denigrating the use of saturated fats mistakenly describe them (and their cousin cholesterol) as artery-clogging. Perhaps this would be true if they were hydrogenated, but just like all other natural foods, saturated fats break down into their original components (mainly smaller fatty acids and glycerol). In my opinion, a better way of looking at saturated fats is as antioxidants because they are very stable fats, which prevent the oxidation of unsaturated fatty acids, fats that are highly prone to rancidity.

Over the years, I have had many clients, family and friends lose weight or overcome conditions such as acne, constipation, joint degeneration, depression and infertility simply by exchanging soybean, canola, corn and other highly processed vegetable oils for schmaltz (chicken fat), lard, butter and even coconut oil (a saturated fat not derived from animals). Despite the list of benefits to eating saturated fats, drug and food processing companies have made trillions of dollars over the years by convincing us these fats cause disease.

When you make the switch to natural saturated fats, seek out *unhydrogenated* versions. If in doubt because of incomplete labeling, you will recognize unhydrogenated fats because they are soft or even semi-liquid at room temperature. Hydrogenated fats remain hard even at temperatures up to approximately 145 degrees. Fats from animals raised on pasture instead of feedlots is best, but as of the writing of this book, I consider *any* unhydrogenated animal fat to be better than any of the cheap vegetable oils that line supermarket and health food store shelves.

Two popular oils that are fine to eat are extra virgin olive oil and sesame oil. Along with a few others, these plant oils have stood the test of time, however, that does not mean that fat consumption should be limited to these. Each oil or fat has different health benefits and temperature thresholds before they produce free radicals, volatile compounds which have a high correlation with soaring cancer rates. So consuming a combination of fats and oils is wise.

As you can imagine, there is a wealth of information and misinformation about fat and cholesterol that are beyond the scope of this book. My intention here is to give you an overview of the reasons natural fats have been included in this book.

WHOLE GRAINS

Unlike the average whole foods nutritionist today, I am not hung up on using whole grains 100% of the time. In the current push to eat more fiber, few people are aware of the fact that massive amounts of fiber can irritate the delicate hair-like projections in the intestines called *villi* and even lead to constipation over time.

Nutrition researchers such as Sally Fallon Morell and Ann Wigmore have touted the importance of soaking or souring grains in an acidic medium (such as water with a touch of yogurt or lemon juice added) before cooking and eating them. Soaking helps to predigest grains and make all of their nutrients more bioavailable. This practice also breaks down the phytic acid in grains, which blocks nutrient absorption, and takes the harsh edge off of fiber, giving whole grain products a better mouth feel and easier transit through the digestive tract.

In my own experience, I have found that people who have suspected that they had gluten intolerance (a mechanical inability to digest the protein gluten in wheat and related grains) have suddenly discovered an ability to digest wheat and other gluten-containing grains properly as long as they are soaked in this manner. I have also noticed that nearly 100% of the people who have reported to me that they suffer from gluten intolerance have spent several months or years eating low-fat diets, high fiber, and/or whole grain foods that have *not* been properly prepared. I believe that it is only a matter of time before a study is performed that proves that depriving the intestines of their preferred food (saturated fat) and the overconsumption of fiber are risk factors for gluten intolerance and even celiac disease (a genetic form of gluten intolerance, which involves a more biochemical reaction to the consumption of gluten-containing grains).

Properly preparing grains does not only apply to wheat, spelt, barley and other gluten-containing grains. It is a good practice for nearly every grain.

On the other hand, brown rice is one grain that does not require soaking prior to cooking. I do, however, find that it has a much more pleasant texture and flavor when soaked in filtered water with a splash of raw apple cider vinegar added to the soaking water.

So when it comes to grains, if you cannot prepare your whole grains properly by soaking them beforehand, I recommend to choose the least processed version you can find. For example, when choosing pasta, the ones I look to first are those made from brown rice, buckwheat or unenriched durum semolina. If you only eat pasta once or twice per month, this is an acceptable compromise food. Anyone suffering from either gluten intolerance or celiac disease would benefit from avoiding semolina, which is a form of wheat.

For piecrust, I use unbleached, unenriched, and unbromated, preferably organic flour. Bleaching, bromating and enriching flour adds many undesirable contaminants to your foods including a host of heavy metals and chemicals.

DAIRY

Dairy has gotten a bad rap over the past few decades. First we were told that it was contributing to excessive weight gain, so we were convinced to consume only low or no fat versions of it. Now it seems that half the population believes that milk is incompatible with human physiology, despite the fact that we are mammals. So they begin drinking fake, highly processed "milks" made from soy, hemp, almonds and rice.

Few have contemplated the fact that our ancestors have consumed milk in one form or another since our early existence. Today, many societies still attribute their longevity to the consumption of dairy products. And while most everybody acknowledges that the French are skinnier and live longer than Americans despite eating plenty of butter and cream sauces, we still choose a tasteless, low-fat lifestyle.

Other people argue that humans are the only mammal that drink milk of another animal past infancy. This popular myth runs rampant among city folk. We are also the only animals that cultivate crops, wear clothing, harness electricity, and watch reruns of *Seinfeld*. So what? We drink other animals' milk because we can and it's good for us. Talk to any dairy farmer and they will tell you that many farm animals crowd around the milking room at milking time to lap up any milk that may spill outside of the room. It's good stuff!

The sad fact is that in the U.S. and increasingly around the world, milk is no longer a whole food. Like most vegetable oils, the milk that lines supermarket shelves is a rancid product that has been treated so as to not reveal its true age. Milk that has been pasteurized is defenseless against pathogenic bacteria such as listeria and *E. coli*. The largest salmonellosis outbreak in U.S. history affected nearly 200,000 people came from *pasteurized* milk produced at one dairy in Illinois. These pasteurized milk outbreaks occur relatively frequently and often involve the death of several people affected.

Homogenized milk is very difficult to digest because the fat molecules in the milk are pushed through screens at high pressure to artificially suspend them in the rest of the milk. As a result, the body has difficulty making sense of these kind of milk molecules when they enter the blood stream and over time may perceive it as a threat. This is likely to be one source of dairy allergies.

Alternatively, if you follow the advice to drink skim milk, you are merely drinking the lactose portion of the milk that has been tampered with. In light of the fact that lactose intolerance seems to be on the rise, I believe it would make more sense to drink the cream and toss the watery blue lactose portion of the milk instead.

On the other hand, *unpasteurized* milk is the way that our ancestors drank milk until a little over 100 years ago. Studies have shown that because it has not had its defenses (enzymes) killed off by the pasteurization process, raw milk can actually kill bacteria on contact. And that cream that I told you to drink in place of the skim portion of the milk? Yep, you guessed it. It can be a source of valuable fat-soluble vitamins and minerals that are very important to the health of your intestinal tract.

Just like with the animal fats from meats, if you are drinking raw milk, the best bet is to get it from pastured animals. Many states allow you to purchase directly from the farm often by belonging to a cow (or goat) share program, where you pay to be part owner of the animal and receive the benefits of what the animal produces. In a few states, you can even purchase this milk in stores. Check http://www.realmilk.org to find raw milk in your area.

SALT

Salt is essential to life. It stimulates the appetite as much as it satisfies the appetite. Salt helps you to digest your food. So adding enough salt to your recipes so that they satisfy your taste buds is important.

That said, it is important to use real salt. I define real salt as any naturally occurring salt that is naturally dehydrated. The two basic types are Himalayan salt, which is mined, and sea salt, which comes from the ocean. Both contain moisture (sea salt more so than mined salt) so it is not uncommon for them to clump slightly in their packaging. They both also contain a wide array of minerals, including the often difficult-to-obtain trace minerals.

On the other hand, regular table salt is a highly refined substance. It contains mainly one mineral — sodium chloride. Unlike natural salts, table salt wreaks havoc on health and is associated with raising blood pressure. In cases where iodine is added to it, the iodine comes in a toxic form that is even more health damaging. Some people mistakenly believe Kosher salt to be a natural salt, but in fact, it is even more highly processed than regular table salt and should be avoided. Coarse sea salt is a much safer alternative to Kosher salt.

Conventional health practitioners make no distinction between the many types of salt on the market and offer only blanket recommendations to avoid or limit salt. This has left many people not only with impaired digestion, but it also leaves food less satisfying. The result of the latter is overeating naturally low sodium foods, namely desserts.

Progressive health practitioners, however, will encourage their patients to consume naturally dried sea salt or Himalayan salt on their food and even in their water. In fact, many have found that unlike regular salt, these natural salts help *lower* blood pressure and improve poor digestion.

Recommendations for my favorite brands of salt and other quality ingredients may be found at the Nutrition Heretic product page (http://nutritionheretic.com/shop).

In the event that you choose to replace any of these ingredient recommendations with conventional ones or you ignore the grain preparation techniques, keep in mind that you may need to adjust liquid requirements and cooking times. With all this in mind, let's get cooking!

BREAKFAST

COCK CONGEE

Serves 6

This nourishing Chinese rice porridge is eaten throughout China for breakfast. It is also considered an appropriate food for babies, the elderly and convalescing individuals. It is a warming, comforting dish on a cold winter day. While the Chinese would use white rice, I like to bump up the nutrition with brown rice. The resulting porridge is not as gluey as when made with white rice, but the flavor is just as rich.

Ingredients:

½ cup long grain brown rice

4 cups filtered water + more as needed

1 quart cock stock

2 cups cock meat reserved from making stock, chopped

2 scallions, finely sliced

sesame oil, to taste

soy sauce or sauce reserved from soy sauce cock, to taste

kimchee (optional)

Soak rice overnight in 4 cups of water. Drain. Place rice and stock in crockpot. Turn to low and cook for 8-12 hours. Replace liquid with filtered water, if necessary. Fifteen minutes before serving, add reserved meat, scallion and sesame oil. Pour into bowls. Serve with soy sauce and/or kimchee.

APPETIZERS

COCKETTES

Serves 6

Some recipes for Spanish croquettes feature a complicated array of ingredients that detract from the delicate poultry flavor. I learned this recipe from the woman I lived with during the year I studied in Spain. These tasty treats were typically served for supper with a bowl of soup or chunk of bread. They are perfect for snacks or filling lunch boxes and can be frozen to make an excellent alternative to processed chicken nuggets. Reheat in oven.

Ingredients:

12 oz. breast meat reserved from making stock, shredded

½ cups unsalted butter

1 large onion, finely chopped

6 Tbs unbleached flour

2 cup milk

rich stock, as needed (see soup section)

½ to 1 cup Manchego cheese, grated

salt to taste

2 eggs, beaten

3 cups whole grain sourdough breadcrumbs

stable oil such as non-hydrogenated coconut or lard for frying*

Melt butter in a large sauté pan. Add onion to pan and cook slowly until translucent. Add breast meat and flour to pan. Stir to mix for approximately 2 minutes. Slowly add milk, stirring all the while to break up any lumps. Gently boil mixture to thicken. If mixture becomes too tough to stir, add some stock a little at a time to loosen it. The mixture should be thick like honey. It should not be too dry. Season with salt to taste. If cheese is used, add it before the salt so that the mixture is not too salty. In general, croquettes should have a delicate milky flavor and not be overly salted. Pour into a pie plate and allow to set in the refrigerator for 2 hours or overnight. It will thicken into a stiff mass. When ready to fry, use an oval tablespoon to cut out a 3-inch long croquette. Dip in beaten egg, then in breadcrumbs. Fry in hot fat over medium heat, turning to brown on all sides. Drain on paper towels. Serve.

* Although not traditional, croquettes may be baked in the oven instead of fried. In that case, make the mixture much dryer before refrigerating or you'll have an oozing mess on your baking sheet. After breading, lay on baking sheet and drizzle with extra virgin olive oil, melted lard or coconut oil. Bake in 350° oven for 30 minutes turning twice to brown on all sides.

WORLD'S BEST PÂTÉ?
– NOT JUST FOR LIVER LOVERS

Serves 8

This is definitely one of those recipes, which proves that if you don't like something, it's because you haven't had it prepared the right way. My husband who had always had an aversion to liver, loves this pâté for breakfast, lunch or as a snack -- so do our children. In fact, this recipe has gotten rave reviews from many pâté connoisseurs as well. It just might be the best recipe in this book. Try it!

Ingredients:

1 lb. chicken and/or rooster livers, deveined

1 large onion or 4 shallots, coarsely chopped

6-8 Tbs unsalted butter at room temperature, preferably raw, cut into chunks

1 tsp dried tarragon

½ tsp paprika

1 tsp Dijon mustard

salt to taste

3 Tbs cognac, armagnac or brandy

Melt 2 tablespoons butter in a medium-sized sauté pan. Add onion or shallot and let cook over medium flame for 10 minutes or until onion becomes slightly translucent. Meanwhile, devein livers, if necessary, making sure to keep them as whole as possible. Remove onion to food processor and purée. If necessary, add a tablespoon or more butter to same pan where you cooked the onion and quickly cook livers over medium-high heat. Add tarragon, paprika and a generous pinch of salt. Add livers to onions in food processor when they are still pink inside, but not too bloody.* Add cognac to pan to remove all the flavorful bits left behind. Reduce to half its volume or flambé by lighting it with a match to remove alcohol completely. While cognac is reducing or flames are dying down, add remaining butter and mustard, pulse ingredients together. Livers should retain some texture. Add reduced cognac to mixture and stir with spatula to melt any remaining chunks of butter. Pour into serving bowl. Excellent on bread, crackers, lettuce or endives, or just eaten alone off the spoon!

* Livers are better a little underdone than over-cooked as they will continue to cook in the food processor. If they cook too much, the end product will taste gritty, not velvety.

Pâté with hard-boiled egg and red onion garnish

SOUPS

COCK STOCK

Makes 4 quarts

This stock is the basis of many delicious soups and savory dishes. I keep plenty on hand for its nutritional benefits and the phenomenal flavor it lends to savory dishes.

Ingredients:

> 1 whole cock, preferably with head and feet on
>
> 1 large onion, roughly chopped
>
> 2 carrots, roughly chopped
>
> 2 ribs celery, roughly chopped
>
> 4 quarts filtered water
>
> 1 Tbs raw cider vinegar
>
> salt to taste

Place all ingredients, except salt, in a large stockpot. Cover with water. Simmer covered for 2 hours over low heat. Lift out cock and remove meat from bones. Reserve meat for use in other recipes. Place bones back in pot and simmer for another 2 hours or more. Add salt 15 minutes before removing from heat. Strain stock, cool, then refrigerate. Remove hardened fat that has accumulated on top and discard. Your stock is now ready for use in other recipes.

TO CLARIFY STOCK

Due to the long simmering, stock tends to be a bit on the cloudy side. If you want a prettier stock suitable for clear soups, you'll want to clarify it. Here's how to do it.

Ingredients:

      4 quarts cooled stock

      2 egg whites

      2 eggshells

Whisk egg whites until frothy. Crush eggshells with your hands and add to beaten whites. Pour the whole mixture into stock then bring to the boil stirring continuously. Allow stock to boil until it foams. Turn off heat and strain stock through several layers of cheesecloth. The resultant clear stock can be used as the basis of elegant dishes such as vichysoisse, consommé, or clear Asian soups.

COCK SOUP

Makes 4 quarts

Ingredients:

1 whole cock, preferably with head and feet on

1 large onion, sliced thinly

2 carrots, peeled and sliced on an angle

2 ribs celery, chopped thin

3 cups assorted diced vegetables (e.g. Leafy cooking greens, string beans, turnips, potatoes or anything lying at the bottom of your refrigerator)

4 quarts filtered water

1 Tbs raw cider vinegar

Sea salt to taste

Place cock, cider vinegar and filtered water into a large stockpot. Simmer covered for one hour over low heat. Remove any scum that accumulates at the top of the stock and discard. Add all vegetables to the pot and continue to cook for another hour. Lift out cock and remove meat from bones. Reserve bones for making stock. Return meat to pot. Add sea salt and stir to dissolve. Serve hot.

VARIATION: MIRACLE COCK SOUP
(FOR GETTING RID OF COLDS FAST!)

Yes, it's a bold claim to suggest that something as simple as a bowl of soup might actually be able to cure the common cold, but I have used this remedy for over 20 years with great success. In fact, I have been able to chase colds and flu away in as little as 2 hours using this concoction followed by a nap under a warm blanket. A few years ago a friend of mine was telling me that chicken soup was not helping her son's cold and fever. I suggested she add the following ingredients to the soup and try again, then having him take a nap in warm bed clothes. Three hours later, she called me to say that his fever had broken and he was acting like his old self.

Additional Ingredients:

  1 inch of fresh ginger, sliced into 5 pieces (warming)

  3 cloves of garlic, smashed (warming and antibiotic properties)

  3 oz. Mung bean noodles (drying — especially for mucous)

Add ginger and garlic to pot along with cock, cider vinegar and filtered water in stockpot. Add mung bean noodles along with sea salt at the end of cooking, just before serving.

SIMPLE DIGESTIVE BROTH

Serves 4

When I lived in Yugoslavia in the 1980s, this soup was often served at the start of the midday meal. So when my mother lost her appetite and started losing too much weight, I knew I had to stimulate her stomach to want more than just the occasional piece of bread. Luckily, before she came for a visit, I had just made a pot of stock. When she arrived, she was barely able to move or interact and was shaking from severe hypoglycemia. After drinking a few cups of this, she left less than 48 hours later moving with less assistance and even had the energy to complain! Keeping with her broth regimen, within a few more days, her mobility continued to improve, she was fully engaging in conversation and most importantly had an appetite!

Ingredients:

> 6 cups cock stock, strained
>
> 1/4 cup broken vermicelli noodles
>
> 2 Tbs parsley, finely chopped
>
> Sea salt to taste

Heat stock in a medium-sized pot. Add vermicelli and cook according to directions (usually 3-4 minutes). Add parsley and salt to taste. Serve warm.

Simple broth revives the dead

CARIBBEAN-STYLE COCK SOUP

Serves 6

Cock soup is a tradition in many countries. As stated in the introduction to this book, it was especially reserved for pregnant women in Jamaican households to ensure the birth of healthy babies. In fact, when my uncle left Jamaica to pursue his fortune in England before sending for his growing family, my grandfather prepared this soup every day for my aunt. It is clear from the beautiful bone structure, straight teeth, clear skin and overall vibrant health of her children that feeding cock soup to pregnant women is the best way to avoid costly visits to the orthopedist, orthodontist, dermatologist and even your regular family doctor. Many modern Jamaicans, however, have forgotten this practice and opt for an MSG-filled dried version widely sold in grocery stores. As a result, younger generations suffer the same deformities and problems of children in industrialized countries.

Ingredients:

1 whole cock

4 quarts filtered water

1 Tbs raw cider vinegar

1/2 lb yucca, diced

1 lb potatoes, diced

1 unripe chayote, diced

1 small onion, diced

2 cloves garlic, smashed

2 carrots, diced

2 ribs celery, chopped thin

5 sprigs fresh or dried thyme

Sea salt to taste

One scotch bonnet pepper, whole and unpunctured

Place cock, cider vinegar and filtered water into a large stockpot. Simmer covered for one hour over low heat. Remove any scum that accumulates at the top of the stock and discard. Add all vegetables and thyme to the pot and continue to cook for another hour. Lift out cock and remove meat from bones. Reserve bones for enriching other batches of stock. Return meat to pot. Add sea salt and whole pepper and stir to dissolve. Be careful not to puncture the pepper or your soup will be too peppery to enjoy. By leaving it whole, you will get the aroma of the pepper, which is much more pleasing. Serve hot. Freeze extra for an easy dinner on a busy night.

Jamaican vegetable market

COCK AVGOLÉMONO

Serves 6

Ingredients:

 1 whole cock

 1 large onion, quartered

 2 carrots, peeled and cut into a few large pieces

 2 quarts filtered water

 1 cup brown rice, soaked in filtered water for at least 2 hours

 3 large eggs

 2 lemons, juiced and strained

 Sea salt to taste

Make a simple stock by placing cock, vegetables and water into a large stock pot. Simmer covered for 3-4 hours over low heat. Remove any scum that accumulates at the top of the stock and discard. Lift out cock and remove meat from bones. Reserve bones for enriching other meat stocks. Return meat to pot of stock. Add rice and cook until rice is tender. Turn off heat.

In a bowl, beat eggs and lemon juice thoroughly to combine. While whisking constantly, ladle in 4 to 5 spoons full of broth. Go slowly so as to "temper" the egg mixture. This will prevent the eggs from curdling. Then slowly pour egg mixture into pot of soup continuing to whisk. Add sea salt and stir to dissolve. Serve hot.

COCK-A-LEEKIE

Serves 6-8

Along with *Coq au Vin*, Cock-A-Leekie is another traditional dish you may have heard of that highlights the flavor of cock. It hails from Scotland where it is said that the resultant soup should be thick and abundant in leeks. The addition of prunes seems to be hotly contested by some, but by others it is considered a must.

Ingredients:

1 whole cock

12 large leeks, thoroughly cleaned*

4 quarts filtered water

1 Scottish bouquet

12 pitted prunes

Jamaica pepper

Sea salt to taste

Place cock in a stock pot with 3 or 4 chopped leeks and Scottish bouquet. Cover in water. Cook for 2 hours or until meat is tender. Remove cock and bouquet from the pot. Add rest of the leeks, cut into one-inch lengths, pepper and salt. Simmer very gently until leeks are very tender. Add prunes half an hour before serving soup. Chop a cup or so of the cock meat to add to the soup. Serve hot.
* To clean leeks, they must have the hairy bottoms removed then slit in half or quartered lengthwise. Blast them as best you can with

running water in between the leaves to remove all the sand and dirt in them. As a precaution, place them in a bowl of water for at least 10 minutes to allow any additional dirt to fall to the bottom so your final dish will not be gritty.

NETTLE KAIL

Serves 6-8

Here is a more obscure traditional Scottish soup that also relies on the cock — in this case a cockerel, which is more tender — as its base ingredient. Typically made in early March when both the young nettles and cockerel were at their best for making this dish, it was said to purify the blood if eaten for three consecutive days. Since nettles are a bit difficult for most people to find, substitute spinach, if you must.

Ingredients:

1 cockerel

3 cloves young garlic or 3 garlic scapes

4 quarts filtered water

1 1/2 cup whole oats or barley, soaked overnight in cold water with 1 Tbs of raw cider vinegar

1 lb young nettles or spinach, thoroughly washed

1/2 cup butter

Sea salt to taste

Mix one cup of the drained oats or barley, half of the butter, 2 cloves of garlic and salt to season. Stuff the cockerel with this mixture. Place bird and the rest of the barley or oats in a large pot and add water. Bring to a boil slowly. Add chopped nettles, the rest of the butter and garlic, and salt to taste. Simmer until meat is tender. Serve hot.

COCK & BEAN SOUP

Serves 4

Ingredients:

2 quarts cock stock

1/2 lb white beans (cannellini or navy, preferably), soaked in filtered water with a pinch of baking soda for 8 hours and drained*

2 cups cock meat left over from making stock

2 cloves garlic, smashed

1 small onion, chopped

1 medium tomato, chopped

1 head of escarole, shredded

Sea salt to taste

After draining and rinsing beans, place them in a pot and cover with at least 2 inches of filtered water. Bring to a boil and cook for about an hour or until beans are soft, but not mushy. Drain beans. In a large soup pot, warm olive oil and add garlic cloves, onion and tomato. When onion is translucent, add stock and escarole. Cook until escarole is wilted. Add beans, meat and salt. Adjust seasoning as necessary. Serve hot.
* A quicker way to soak beans is to place them in a pot covered with filtered water. Bring water to a boil for 5 minutes. Turn off heat and add a pinch of baking soda. Allow to sit for one hour. Then drain and proceed with recipe.

SALAD
&
SANDWICHES

COCK & WHITE BEAN SALAD

Serves 6

It is important to remember whenever cooking beans that the initial soaking water must be drained and rinsed before the actual cooking. This removes the gassiness from the beans and makes eating them a pleasant experience instead of an embarrassing one.

Ingredients:

1/2 lb white beans (cannellini or navy, preferably), soaked in filtered water with a pinch of baking soda for 8 hours and drained*

2 cups cock meat left over from making stock, chopped

1 shallot, thinly sliced

1/2 cup celery, chopped

1/4 cup red wine or sherry vinegar

1/4 cup or more extra virgin olive oil

1 small bunch of parsley, chopped

Sea salt and white pepper, to taste

After draining and rinsing beans, place them in a pot and cover with at least 2 inches of filtered water. Bring to a boil and cook for about an hour or until beans are soft, but not mushy. Drain beans and place in a bowl. While still warm, add shallot, celery, red wine vinegar, olive oil, salt and pepper. Toss to coat. Add chopped parsley and meat. Toss again. If mixture seems dry, add more olive oil. Serve slightly warm with crusty sourdough bread or serve on lettuce leaves.

* A quicker way to soak beans is to place them in a pot covered with filtered water. Bring water to a boil for 5 minutes. Turn off heat and add a pinch of baking soda. Allow to sit for one hour. Then drain and proceed with recipe.

COCK SALAD SANDWICHES

Serves

Ingredients:

  2 cups cock meat left over from making stock, chopped

  2 scallions, chopped fine

  1/2 cup celery, chopped fine

  2 Tbs chopped walnuts

  1/2 cup mayonnaise (see Basics section)

  Sea salt and white pepper, to taste

Mix all ingredients in a medium bowl. Add more mayonnaise, if mixture seems dry. Serve on toasted sourdough bread or on lettuce leaves for a low carbohydrate alternative

COCK UNDER WRAPS

Serves 4

It may seem like there are a lot of opposing flavors going on in this wrap, but the key to making this work is to use the cheese, pepper and tomato rather sparingly, as accents to the flavor of the pesto.

Ingredients:

> 2 cups cock meat left over from making stock, chopped
>
> 1/2 cup pesto sauce (see Basics section)
>
> 1 red pepper, roasted and sliced thinly
>
> Sun-dried tomatoes packed in extra virgin olive oil, sliced thinly
>
> Fresh mozzarella, thinly sliced or shredded
>
> 1 small head crisp lettuce leaves, shredded
>
> Your favorite tortilla wrap — preferably sourdough or sprouted

Mix the meat and pesto in a medium bowl. Add more pesto, if mixture seems dry; more meat if the mixture seems too wet. Please a scoop of the mixture to one side of your tortilla wrap in a straight line. Add a few strips of tomato and red pepper on top of the meat mixture. Sprinkle with cheese. Coat with lettuce leaves. Pull the edge closest to where the bulk of the filling is and wrap over the filling. Fold in the top and bottom of the tortilla over the filling. Continue rolling toward the empty side of the tortilla until fully wrapped. Eat!

PASTA & RICE

LINGUINE WITH COCK IN LEMON CREAM SAUCE

Serves 8 as a first course

Most packs of pasta suggest to serve a quarter pound of pasta per person. This is entirely too much to consume in one sitting. Italians rarely eat large portions of pasta as their main meal, but as a course that makes up the meal. My suggestion is to follow this dish with a nice refreshing garden salad and a glass of wine.

Ingredients:

1 lb. dried linguine, cooked according to manufacturer's directions

2 Tbs butter

3 shallots finely chopped

2 cups heavy cream (not ultra-pasteurized)

1 lb. cock meat reserved from making stock, chopped

Juice of one lemon

Salt and ground white pepper to taste

In a large sauté pan, melt butter over medium heat. Add shallots and cook until translucent. Be careful not to brown. Next add heavy cream. Bring mixture to a boil. Allow sauce to thicken slightly. Add cock meat and lemon juice. Continue to warm through and adjust seasonings. Thicken sauce a bit more if necessary. You want the final sauce to coat the pasta, but still remain relatively loose. Add freshly drained (not rinsed) linguine to the sauce. Stir to blend. Use a little of the linguine's cooking water to thin the sauce, if it seems too thick. Serve hot.

COCKED UP PASTA PESTO

Serves 8 as a first course

I recently made this dish for a potluck party, where it was one of the first dishes to disappear even though it was at the far end of the table. The addition of cock meat is a delicious in this traditional version of pasta alla pesto.

As stated in the previous pasta recipe, even though it is recommended on most packages of pasta, a pound of pasta is an excessive amount of carbohydrate for four people to eat. Instead, make this for eight people or divide it in half and make for only four. Serve with a garden salad.

Ingredients:

1 lb dried pasta (long or tubular), cooked according to manufacturer's directions (see procedure)

1 recipe pesto sauce (see Basics section)

2 large potatoes, peeled and diced

1/2 lb string beans, trimmed and chopped into 2-inch sticks

1 lbs cock meat reserved from making stock, chopped

8 egg yolks to serve

Salt and ground white pepper to taste

Warm serving eight serving bowls in oven set to 150 degrees. Meanwhile, boil pasta in a large pot of well-salted, boiling water. When the pasta has approximately 7 minutes left of cooking, add potatoes. When pasta and potatoes have approximately 2 minutes of cooking left, add in string beans. Drain when string beans are bright green and tender. Do not discard pasta water yet. Toss meat in with pasta and vegetables. Add pesto. One cup at first and gradually add more until well coated, but not dripping with oil. Thin slightly with a bit of the cooking water, if necessary so that pasta is not too sticky. Serve immediately in pre-warmed bowls with one egg yolk on the top of each serving.

PASTA IN A COCKY TOMATO SAUCE

Serves 8 as a first course

As stated in the other pasta recipes, even though it is recommended on most packages of pasta, a pound of pasta is an excessive amount of carbohydrate for four people to eat. Instead, make this for eight people or divide it in half and make for only four. Serve with a garden salad.

Ingredients:

1 lb dried pasta (long or tubular), cooked according to manufacturer's directions

3 Tbs extra virgin olive oil

1 large onion, chopped

2 25-oz. cans of tomato puree

1 cup cock stock

1 tsp dried oregano

1 bay leaf

1 lb cock meat reserved from making stock, chopped

2 bell peppers, sliced (optional)

Sea salt to taste

In a large heavy-bottomed pan, sauté onion in olive oil until onion is translucent. Add tomato puree, stock and herbs. Cook on medium heat partially covered. Add meat and adjust seasonings. Toss in optional peppers and cook until peppers become slightly limp. When pasta is done to the al dente stage, drain without rinsing and add to sauce. Cook quickly over high heat to allow pasta to absorb the flavors of the sauce. Serve hot.

Pasta in a cocky tomato sauce improvised as a stew

COCK FRIED RICE

Serves 8

Ingredients:

3 eggs, beaten

1 tsp toasted sesame oil

pinch fine sea salt

4 cups cold leftover brown or white rice

2 Tbs soy sauce

3 Tbs non-hydrogenated lard, coconut or peanut oil

1 cup cock meat leftover from making stock, chopped

½ cup frozen peas

fine sea salt to taste

2 scallions, sliced into ½ pieces on a diagonal

In a bowl, beat eggs with sesame oil and pinch of salt. Heat a wok or large frying pan. When it just begins to smoke, add one tablespoon of the lard or oil. Add eggs and mix in wok so it lightly cooks evenly in a flat layer. Remove to plate. Eggs should still be slightly wet. Roll egg and slices into strips. Add remaining lard or oil to wok. When hot, add rice and quickly begin to stir so it heats evenly. Sprinkle with soy sauce to moisten. Add meat and peas. Continue to cook until peas have thawed. Sprinkle with salt, if necessary. Add scallions and mix. Cook another minute. Serve hot.

PAELLA CON COCK

Serves 8

Here is another recipe I learned from the *Señora* I lived with in Spain. There are several differences to my recipe, but the results are still better than most of what you get outside of Valencia, Spain – the home of paella. The first difference is that I make mine with brown rice instead of the white paella rice called *Bomba*. Another difference is that it is usually made with a young chicken, instead of a cock or stewing hen that requires long cooking. My final violation of this dish is covering the paella to thoroughly cook the rice, but I assure you, when using brown rice this is necessary and will not make the final result unpleasant. Other than that, there is no set recipe for the variety of meat that paella can contain. So use your imagination with ingredients such as mussels, clams, codfish, rabbit, and ham.

Ingredients:

> 3 cups short grain brown rice, soaked for 2 hours in 6 cups water with 1 Tbs raw cider vinegar
>
> 3 Tbs extra virgin olive oil
>
> 1 small onion, finely chopped
>
> 1 small tomato, finely chopped
>
> 1 clove garlic, finely chopped
>
> 1 chorizo sausage, cut into ½" slices
>
> 1 cock, cut into 8 pieces or meat left over from making

stock

water or stock

large pinch of saffron, rubbed

1 tsp smoked paprika

sea salt to taste

1 cup raw shrimp, shelled and deveined

1 roasted red pepper, sliced into strips lengthwise

½ cup frozen peas

2 hard-boiled eggs, sliced lengthwise into quarters

1 lemon cut into wedges

In a large sauté pan or *paellera*, heat olive oil over medium. Add onion, tomato and garlic. Cook gently so they wilt, but do not brown. Brown chorizo in the pan, then remove to platter. If using raw cock meat, sprinkle with salt and add it to the pan. Brown the meat on all sides. Remove to small stockpot and pour in water or stock. Simmer until meat is nearly tender, about 40 minutes. Add drained rice to oil in sauté pan. Cook over medium heat, stirring constantly to coat with oil. Add a few more tablespoons of olive oil if necessary. In about 5 minutes when rice begins to smell fragrant, pour in all the stock from the stockpot. Bring to a boil, continuing to stir rice occasionally. Add saffron, paprika, and salt (if necessary). Nestle meat neatly amongst the rice. Simmer. When liquid has reduced until it barely covers the rice, place sausage, shrimp, roasted peppers and peas into pan. If using meat reserved from making stock, add it now. Use the back of a flat spoon to gently incorporate these ingredients into rice. Allow top of rice to dry, then cover. If you do not have a cover large enough to cover the pan, then cover with a layer of paper towels followed by several sheets of newspaper. Rice is done when no water remains, but note that the end result will have a light gravy. Decorate with eggs and lemon neatly arranged on top. Serve hot.

Perfectly prepared paella

RISOTTO

Serves 10

Risotto is an Italian rice dish traditionally made with chicken stock. In this case, we use cock stock, which as stated before has a richer flavor and a more robust nutritional profile. It is considered a bit of a sacrilege to reheat risotto, but in the following recipe, you'll find a yummy way to use any leftovers.

Ingredients:

1 lb. risotto rice (arborio or carnaroli)

1 Tbs extra virgin olive oil

3 Tbs butter

1 shallot or small onion, finely chopped

1 small tomato, finely chopped

1 clove garlic, finely chopped

1 cup dry white wine

5-6 cups hot cock stock

1/2 cup frozen peas (optional)

2 cups cock meat, chopped (optional)

1/4 cup grated hard cheese such as Parmagiano Reggiano or romano

2-4 Tbs butter

In a large sauté pan, heat olive oil over medium. Add butter to melt, then add onion, tomato and garlic. Cook gently so they wilt, but do not brown. Add rice dry (without washing). Stir to coat rice in butter and olive oil. After about 2 minutes, add wine. Stir frequently with a wooden spoon. When wine has evaporated, begin adding stock, one cup at a time, stirring between additions and allowing the rice to absorb the liquid before adding more. Keep adding stock until the rice is cooked, but has not flowered. Do not allow all the stock to absorb at this stage. Leave it rather loose in texture before adding optional peas and cheese. Stir in gently. Dot with butter and fold in. Serve hot.

RISOTTO COCK BALLS

Makes 15 balls

This is a great way to use up leftover risotto which would be too thick and clumpy to enjoy compared to when it is freshly prepared. This is so delicious, in fact, that you may find yourself making risotto simply to have leftovers for this dish. They make a great appetizer or snack at a cocktail party!

Ingredients:

3 cups leftover risotto

1 or 2 large eggs

1/2 cup cock meat, chopped

1/2 cup mozzarella or fontina cheese, chopped

Bread crumbs (optional)

Unhydrogenated, pastured lard or extra virgin olive oil for light frying

In a large bowl, mix risotto with egg. If mixture seems too dry, add another egg. Mixture should be rather firm so that it holds together, but eggy enough that the egg holds the mixture together during frying. Form a 3" disk in one hand. Place a few pieces of meat and cheese in the middle. Bring the edges of the rest of the rice mixture up and around the filling to close. You should now have a risotto ball. Lightly fry in oil or lard. Serve hot.

COCK WITH RICE

Serves 6

Usually this French dish is called *Poule au Riz* because it would be made with a stewing hen, which is another tough bird. Dishes like this underscore the simplicity of French cooking and the fact that you can eat well with a minimum of hands-on prep work, ingredients and skill. Replace the cock or stewing hen with diced pieces of chicken (a fryer or spring chicken) and you have the perfect meal for a camping trip.

Ingredients:

1 cock, whole

3 quarts filtered water

1 carrot, sliced

1 medium onion, sliced

2 cups rice, washed

A few sprigs of fresh herbs such as thyme, rosemary, parsley, or bay leaf

Sea salt to taste

Place cock in a large pan or pot. Add water, vegetables, herbs and salt. Cover and simmer for 2 hours or until meat is tender. Add rice and cook for another half hour until rice is cooked through.

TURKISH-STYLE COCK WITH RICE

Serves 8

This dish is very similar to Paella, but instead of saffron and sausage, you will add pine nuts, raisins, and dill. It's equally delicious.

Ingredients:

3 cups short grain brown rice, soaked for 2 hours in 6 cups water with 1 Tbs raw cider vinegar

3 Tbs extra virgin olive oil or butter

1 medium onion, finely chopped

1 medium tomato, finely chopped

1 bunch fresh dill, finely chopped

1 cock, cut into 8 pieces or meat left over from making stock

1 cock's liver, diced (optional)

water or stock

2 Tbs pine nuts or almonds

2 Tbs raisins

1 large onion, sliced thin

sea salt to taste

In a large sauté pan or *paellera*, heat 2 tablespoons of the oil or butter over medium heat. Add onion and tomato. Cook gently so they wilt, but do not brown. If using raw cock meat, sprinkle with salt and add it to the pan. Brown the meat on all sides. Remove to small stockpot and pour in water or stock. Simmer until meat is nearly tender, about 40 minutes. Add drained rice and pine nuts to oil in sauté pan. Cook over medium heat, stirring constantly to coat with oil and lightly brown the pine nuts. Add a few more tablespoons of olive oil if necessary. In about 5 minutes when rice begins to smell fragrant, pour in all the stock from the stockpot. Bring to a boil, continuing to stir rice occasionally. Add salt, if desired. Nestle meat neatly amongst the rice. If using reserved meat from making stock, add it now. Simmer. When liquid has reduced until it barely covers the rice, cover the pan with a tight-fitting lid and allow to cook over low heat or in the oven for 20 minutes or until done. While rice is cooking, cook onions in a small sauté pan with remaining oil or butter over medium-high heat. Cook past the golden stage until the sugars in the onion begin to take on a caramel color. Stir periodically so as not to burn. When fully caramelized, add to rice dish and stir in. Serve hot.

Turkish-Style Cock with Rice

ENTREES

COCK PAPRIKASH

Serves 6

For some unknown reason, many people say that Czech food is boring and tasteless. Paprikash is just one of many hearty and tasty dishes I enjoyed when I went to Prague for my honeymoon. This dish or some permutation of it makes a relatively frequent appearance in my kitchen.

Ingredients:

    1 cock, cut into 8 pieces

    2 T butter

    1 onion, minced

    1 tsp caraway seeds

    2 cups filtered water or cock stock

    1 cup heavy cream

    1 tsp sweet paprika

    salt and pepper, to taste

Melt butter in large sauté pan. When hot, place meat in pan. Brown on all sides sprinkling with salt and pepper. Remove meat to plate. Add onion and caraway seeds to pan and cook until soft. Return meat to pan along with stock. Cover and simmer on low for one hour and fifteen minutes or until meat is tender. Turn up heat to high, then add heavy cream and paprika. Boil until sauce is reduced enough to coat the back of a spoon. Serve hot with mashed potatoes or slices of sourdough bread.

BBQ CROCK POT COCK

Serves 6

Crock pots are a great timesaver that not enough people use on a regular basis even though they complain about the lack of time to cook. Here is a wonderful recipe to come home to after a long day of work. Serve with a salad, sautéed greens and a small piece of cornbread or over rice.

Ingredients:

> 1 cock, cut into 8 pieces
>
> Barbecue sauce to coat (see below)
>
> Sea salt and pepper, to taste

Place pieces of meat in the crock pot. Cover with barbecue sauce. Cook for 2-3 hours.

BARBECUE SAUCE

Ingredients:

> 3 Tbs extra virgin olive oil
>
> 1 medium onion, finely chopped
>
> 4 cloves garlic, minced
>
> 1/2 cup tomato paste
>
> 1/2 cup tomato purée

1/2 cup raw cider vinegar

1 Tbs blackstrap molasses

3 Tbs naturally dried cane sugar such as Rapadura or Sucanat

2 tsp hot paprika

1 Tbs sea salt

In a medium-sized pot, warm olive oil over medium heat. Add onion and garlic. Sauté for 5 minutes until slightly soft. Add remaining ingredients and cook, uncovered until thick. Purée in a blender.

COCK WITH WINE

Serves 6

Coq au vin is a popular French recipe. Although it traditionally used rooster as its main ingredient, more modern recipes are more likely to call for a young spring female chicken. However, due to the long cooking process and the bold flavors involved, I still prefer it with a good hardy cock.

Ingredients:

   1 cock, cut into 8 pieces

   unbleached flour for dusting

   5 slices bacon, chopped

   2 Tbs butter (optional)

   ¼ cup cognac

   1 cup pearl onions

   1 Tbs tomato paste

   1 *bouquet garni* (see Basics section)

   1 clove garlic, mashed

   2 cup red wine such as Beaujolais

   salt to taste

Sauté bacon in large frying pan to render fat. Add butter to melt. Sauté onions in hot fat to brown on all sides. Remove to plate. Dust meat with flour and brown in remaining fat over medium heat. Off heat, add cognac then stand back and carefully light with a match. When flames die down, add garlic, tomato paste, herbs and wine. Cover and cook for one hour or until meat is tender. Uncover, add salt and continue to cook allowing sauce to thicken slightly. Serve hot.

COCK WITH BEER

Serves 6

While nearly everybody has heard of *coq au vin*, few are familiar with its Flemish relative *coq à la bière*. As the name suggests, the rich wine sauce is replaced with a beer sauce. The results are equally spectacular.

Ingredients:

> 1 cock, cut into 8 pieces
>
> unbleached flour for dusting
>
> 5 slices fatty bacon, chopped
>
> 2 Tbs butter
>
> 2 bottles of blond beer
>
> 1 cup pearl onions
>
> 1 1/2 cup button mushrooms
>
> 25 black peppercorns
>
> 25 juniper berries
>
> A pinch of sugar
>
> salt to taste

AROMATIC VEGETABLE MIX

1 lb carrots, peeled and sliced

1 lb onions, quartered

1/2 head garlic, peeled and lightly smashed

1 *bouquet garni* (see Basics section)

2 tomatoes, quartered

In a large heavy bottomed casserole or pan with tight fitting lid, sauté bacon in large frying pan to render fat. Remove 2 tablespoons bacon fat and reserve. Add one tablespoon butter to melt. Sauté cock until well browned on all sides. Remove to plate. Next add vegetables for the aromatic garnish to casserole and allow to cook 5 to 10 minutes.

Return cock pieces to casserole, dust with flour and place in a 250 degree oven for 10 minutes. Remove from oven and place over high heat on stove. Immediately add both bottles of beer. Add *bouquet garni*, peppercorns, juniper berries and salt. Cover with tight fitting lid and return to oven for 1 1/2 to 2 hours.

In a sauté pan, add reserved bacon fat and second tablespoon of butter. Add mushrooms and pearl onions whole. Sprinkle with sugar and a pinch of salt. Cook over high heat and stir frequently to prevent burning. Add a few tablespoons of water, then allow to cook down and caramelize.

When meat is cooked through and tender, remove from oven and arrange pieces on a warm serving plate. Add the mushroom and pearl onion mix, then strain the beer sauce over everything. Serve hot.

VARIATION:

Before adding the beer sauce over the meat and mushroom mixture, return it to the stove and add a cup of crème fraîche to it. Stir vigorously with a whisk. When slightly thickened, pour this sauce over the meat and mushrooms. Serve immediately.

COCK WITH CIDER

Serves 6

Another cousin of *coq au vin*, *coq au cidre* is also a delicious variation on this classic.

Ingredients:

1 cock, whole

1 lbs. Granny Smith or other sour apples, peeled and sliced thin

2 Tbs butter

2 cloves, lightly crushed

1/2 tsp dried thyme

3 shallots, finely chopped

1/2 bottle French cider

Sea salt to taste

1 cup heavy cream, not ultra-pasteurized

Stuff cock with 1/2 of the apples. In a large pan, melt butter and add meat. Brown on all sides for about 20 minutes total. Add shallots to pan and cook until translucent. Add rest of remaining ingredients, except cream. Bring to the boil, then reduce heat and cook for one hour or until meat is tender. Remove meat to a warmed platter. Add cream to sauce, bring to boil and cook until reduced by one third. Pour sauce over meat and serve hot.

COCK WITH WHITE WINE

Serves 6

You've seen it cooked in red wine, beer and cider. Now we have a simple white wine version. Enjoy.

Ingredients:

1 large cock, cut into 8 serving pieces

4 Tbs butter, unhydrogenated lard, or chicken fat

2 medium onions, chopped

1 medium carrot, chopped

1 celery stick, chopped

1 b*ouquet garni* (see Basics section)

1 Tbs unbleached flour

1/4 tsp paprika

1 cup cock stock (see Basics section)

1 cup dry white wine

1/4 cup dry white vermouth (optional)

7 oz button mushrooms, cleaned and chopped

Pinch cayenne pepper

Sea salt to taste

In a large pan, melt half of the butter over medium heat. Add the meat and brown on all sides. Remove to a platter. To the pan, add onion, carrot, celery and *bouquet garni*. Cook slowly, stirring frequently until the vegetables are limp, but not browned. Dust with flour and allow the flour to brown slightly, while continuing to stir. Add stock and wine. Let cook 20 minutes on a low flame. Meanwhile, in a separate sauté pan, sauté mushrooms in remaining butter. Set aside.

Once the sauce is cooked, strain it through a fine-mesh strainer, pressing well to remove as much of the sauce as possible. Return the meat, strained sauce and mushrooms to the large pan. Sprinkle with cayenne pepper and add salt. Cover and simmer over a low flame for an hour or until meat is tender. Ten minutes before serving, add the optional vermouth. Cook for 10 minutes boiling slightly. Serve hot.

COCK WITH PEPPERS

Serves 6

Ingredients:

1 cock, cut into 8 serving pieces

2 Tbs butter

2 Tbs extra virgin olive oil

1/2 cup dry white wine

2 cups cock stock or water

2 medium onions, sliced thin

1 clove garlic, smashed

6 bell peppers, sliced thin

Several sprigs of fresh thyme

Sea salt to taste

In a large pan, sauté meat in butter. Brown on all sides. Add cognac and cook to evaporate. Next add stock and salt. Cover and simmer on a low flame for an hour or until meat is tender. Open cover and let stock reduce to a light syrup stage. Meanwhile, in a separate pan, heat olive oil and sauté onions, garlic, thyme and peppers. Cook well, but do not allow to become too limp so that they begin to disintegrate. Add pepper mixture to meat. Stir well and adjust seasoning. Serve hot.

SUPREME COCK

Yet another testament to how well the French do cock.

Serves 4

Ingredients:

Meat of one cock reserved from making stock (see Basics section)

2 Tbs butter

4 Tbs unbleached flour

1/4 cup dry sherry

3 cups cock stock (see Basics section)

1 cup mushrooms, chopped

2 Tbs heavy cream

In a sauce pan, melt butter over medium heat. Add unbleached flour and stir frequently to mix. When flour is slightly browned, add sherry and cook to evaporate. Next, add stock a 1/2 cup at a time to blend. Add mushrooms and cream. When thickened enough to coat the back of a spoon, turn off heat. Add meat to sauce to heat through. Serve immediately.

COCK AND DUMPLINGS

Serves 4

Otherwise known as chicken and dumplings, this classic American dish is a great one-pot meal, which naturally lends itself to the long cooking time required by rooster meat.

Ingredients:

Meat of one cock reserved from making stock, chopped (see Basics section)

4 Tbs butter, unhydrogenated lard, or *schmaltz* (chicken fat)

8 Tbs unbleached flour

1/4 tsp paprika

1 quart cock stock (see Basics section)

1/2 cup heavy cream, *not* ultra-pasteurized

Sea salt to taste

In a large pan, melt butter over medium heat. Add unbleached flour and stir frequently to mix. When flour is slightly browned, add stock and paprika. Bring to the boil, stirring frequently. Reduce heat and continue stirring occasionally for about 10 minutes until you have a thick, smooth sauce. Add meat, cream and salt. Spoon dumpling batter on top of bubbling meat mixture. Cover and "bake" for 10-15 minutes until dumplings are cooked through. Serve immediately.

DUMPLINGS

Ingredients:

2 cups unbleached flour

1 tsp sea salt

1 Tbs baking powder (see Basics)

1 Tbs unhydrogenated lard or butter

3/4 cup cold whole milk

Mix dry ingredients in a large bowl. Slowly add milk and stir with a fork to blend well. To prevent sticking, use a teaspoon dipped in cold water to spoon dumplings onto meat mixture.

COCK COMBS AND WATTLES (CIBREO)

Serves 4

Traditional cuisines make use of every part of the animal. There is no waste. *Cibreo*, a traditional Tuscan dish, is a dish that makes use of the crests and wattles of the cock. It is often served as a main course. Unlike the cock's muscle meat, it does not take two hours to cook. A good side dish would be sautéed zucchini, or buttered carrots or string beans.

Ingredients:

1/2 lb cock crests and wattles

1/4 lb cock livers, chopped into small pieces

2 egg yolks

1/2 lemon

1 onion, grated

2 sage leaves

2 cups of hot cock stock

2 Tbs butter

Sea salt to taste

Clean crests and wattles, then boil them for half an hour. Peel. Meanwhile, heat butter in a large frying pan. Add onion and sage. Sauté until golden brown. Add crests and wattles along with 1/2 cup of stock. Cook for 20 minutes then add livers. Mix lemon juice with egg yolks. With crest mixture off the heat, slowly add yolk mixture in stirring quickly to prevent yolks from cooking. Add salt, then return pan to low heat for a few minutes without boiling to bring the flavors together. Serve hot.

GUMBO

Serves 6

Gumbo is like barbecue. There are as many variations as there are people. Some have okra or tomatoes, others do not. I believe that every version I have seen has some form of seafood or sausage, but then again, I have also seen basic recipes that do not feature either. This is my version with…. Well, you know!

Ingredients:

  1 cock, cut into 8 serving pieces

  4 Tbs unhydrogenated lard or fat of nitrate-free bacon

  1 large onion, chopped

  4 quarts cock stock or water, heated

  2 Tbs parsley, chopped

  2 Tbs scallion, chopped

  Several sprigs of fresh thyme or 1 tsp dried thyme

  1 lb smoked, nitrate-free sausage or ham, sliced

  1 pint oysters

  1 Tbs gumbo filé powder

  1 clove garlic smashed

  Sea salt and pepper to taste

In a large, heavy-bottomed pot, sauté meat in lard to brown on all sides. Add onion and cook until soft. Cover and cook for about 10 minutes stirring occasionally to prevent sticking. Add stock, parsley, scallion, garlic, thyme, salt and pepper. Cover again and cook over low heat for one hour or until meat is tender. Add sausage and cook for 10 minutes. Next add oysters and their liqueur slowly while stirring. Cook for 10 minutes longer before serving.

COCK POT PIE

Serves 8

It takes no more time to make two of these as it would to make one. Freeze the extra one for fast Friday night meal. Leftovers are great reheated and placed in a thermos for a warming and nourishing lunch the next day.

Ingredients:

3 Tbs butter

Cock meat reserved from making stock, chopped

1 onion, diced

2 stalks celery, diced

1 large carrots, diced

2 cups diced, firm vegetables such as parsnips, rutabagas, string beans, potatoes

½ cup peas, lima beans and/or sweet corn

3 Tbs unbleached flour

1 quart stock

1 Tbs dried sage

1 bay leaf

salt to taste

One recipe pie crust (see Basics section)

Preheat oven to 350° F. In a large sauté pan, sauté vegetables and cock meat in butter for two minutes over medium heat. Sprinkle mixture with flour and continue to stir another minute. Add hot stock and boil 10 minutes to thicken. Pour into two 10-inch pie pans. Cover each with a layer of pie crust. Crimp edges and make deep slashes in top of pie to allow air through when mixture beneath boils during baking. Place pies on baking sheet to catch any drippings, then place in oven. Bake for 30 minutes or until nicely browned on top. Makes 2 10-inch pies.

Pot pie fresh from the oven

COCK & PILAF IN PHYLLO

Serves 8

This rich and savory dish is great as a snack or for a party. If eating with a meal, serve following a bowl of any of the soups in this book along with a fresh salad.

You must work quickly when using phyllo dough or yufka. These thin sheets dry out quickly and will become brittle and break. To keep this from happening, place a slightly damp cloth over the unused portions while buttering and layering in the baking dish.

Ingredients:

   1/2 cup + 3 Tbs butter, melted

   6 sheets phyllo pastry or 1 1/2 large yufka sheets, cut into squares

   Cock meat reserved from making stock, chopped

   4 cups rice, cooked

   1 onion, diced

   3 large carrots, diced

   1 cup frozen or fresh peas

   1 cup fresh dill, chopped

   salt to taste

Preheat oven to 350° F. In a small sauté pan, melt 3 tablespoons butter. Sauté onion and carrots then set aside. While mixture is sautéing, butter a 12" diameter pie dish or frying pan. Line dish with one sheet of phyllo pastry that has been cut into a square that will hang over the sides of your baking dish. Brush pastry with butter, then lay another piece of phyllo on top, turning slightly so that the pastry fans out. Repeat buttering and layering with 2 more pieces of the pastry. Next, layer rice, vegetables and meat into pastry. Cover the top with remaining pastry, buttering in between. Fold over hanging corners of the pastry lining the pan and seal by brushing with butter. Bake about 30-40 minutes until top and bottom are golden brown. Remove from oven and let sit for 5 to 10 minutes. Place a large serving plate over the pie dish and invert so that the pie is removed to the plate. Serve at once.

COCK IN A BLANKET (BÖREK)

Börek (pronounced BEUR-ek) is a guilty pleasure that I rarely make at home in the U.S., but will buy in shops when visiting Turkey or Eastern European countries where they use real butter between the layers. It takes its place nicely at breakfast alongside some hard-boiled eggs and black kalamata olives.

The yufka or phyllo in Europe has a lovely texture compared to their American counterparts. You must work quickly when using phyllo dough or yufka. These thin sheets dry out quickly and will become brittle and break. To keep this from happening, place a slightly damp cloth over the unused portions while buttering and layering in the baking dish.

Ingredients:

1/2 cup butter, melted

12 sheets phyllo pastry or 6 large yufka sheets

3 Tbs extra virgin olive oil

2 large onions, diced

6 oz. tomato puree

1 cup cock stock

Cock meat reserved from making stock, chopped

1 cup flat leaf parsley, chopped

salt to taste

Preheat oven to 350° F. Sauté onions in olive oil in a large pan. Add puree, stock and salt. Reduce until sauce is thick, but not dry. You do not want a watery sauce. Add chopped meat and parsley. Mix with the sauce and set aside.

Butter a 12" x 14" baking dish. Line dish with one sheet of phyllo allowing it to hang over the sides. Follow with more butter and another layer of phyllo. Do this 2 more times for a total of 4 sheets of phyllo. Next add a layer of the meat mixture. Repeat alternating 4 layers of phyllo with melted butter. Add another layer of the meat mixture. Then alternate the last 4 layers of phyllo and butter on top. Brush the top with the rest of the butter. Bake about 30-40 minutes in oven until top is golden brown. Remove from oven and let cool slightly. Place a serving platter on top and invert börek onto platter. Cut into squares to serve.

SOY SAUCE COCK

Serves 6

My father got very sentimental when I first made this dish for him. His father, who was originally from China, was apparently a very good cook and organized Chinese banquets in Jamaica, where my father was born. This dish reminded him of the meals grandpa would make.

The remaining sauce in the pot may be frozen and used for the next time you make this delicious dish. You can also use it to flavor stir fries or in as an at table seasoning for my congee recipe at breakfast.

Ingredients:

1 whole cock

2 cups soy sauce

filtered water

½ cup Shao Hsing rice wine

¾ cups rock sugar or brown sugar

4 pieces star anise

1 tsp Szechuan peppercorns

1 four-inch piece ginger, cut into large slices

5 stalks scallion, cut into   four-inch lengths

Place all ingredients, except cock, in a large pot or wok. Simmer gently until sugars are dissolved. Add cock, breast-side down. Add filtered water to cover, raising heat to bring to gentle boil. At the boil, reduce heat to low, cover and simmer for one hour or until meat is tender. Lift cock out of sauce to serving platter. Cut into serving pieces. Remove ¼ cup of remaining sauce from pot. Taste for saltiness. If too salty, dilute with hot water. Serve cock over steamed brown rice with sauce on side.

CREAMY COCK IN COCONUT MILK (GUINATAAN)

Serves 6

Guinataan is a traditional Filipino dish. If you cannot get cream of coconut, you can use a second can of coconut milk that has been sitting still for several hours. Simply skim the thick cream off the top.

Ingredients:

 1 whole cockerel, cut into 8 serving pieces

 3/4 cup raw palm or cider vinegar

 1 can full-fat, additive free coconut milk

 4 cloves garlic, crushed

 1 1/2 inches ginger, peeled and sliced

 1/2 tsp black peppercorns, crushed

 1 tsp fermented soy sauce

 1 fresh hot chili pepper

 1/4 cup cream of coconut (available at Caribbean grocers)

 Sea salt to taste

Marinate meat along with garlic, ginger, cider vinegar and peppercorns for 10 minutes in a bowl. Pre-heat a soup pot. Add marinated meat and coconut milk to warm pot. Simmer for one hour or until meat is tender. In the last 5 minutes of cooking, add the soy sauce and cream of coconut. Stir to thicken the sauce. Adjust seasoning with salt.

COCK ADOBO

Serves 6

Adobo is one of the most popular Filipino dishes and so easy to make. All of my Filipino friends say they make it on a weekly basis. While it typically uses a female chicken (like so many other dishes), the long cooking time makes it a good candidate for replacing the hen with her male counterpart.

Ingredients:

> 1 cock, cut into 8 serving pieces
>
> 1/2 cup coconut oil, lard or chicken fat
>
> 1 cup raw palm, cane or cider vinegar
>
> 1 cup fermented soy sauce
>
> 1/2 head garlic, crushed
>
> 1 large onion, chopped
>
> 1 tsp black peppercorns, crushed
>
> 2 bay leaves

Marinate meat in vinegar, soy sauce, peppercorns and bay leaves for 2 hours. In a large pan, sauté garlic and onion in coconut oil until translucent. Add meat and its marinade to the pan. Cook covered for one hour or until meat is tender. Remove cover and cook another half hour or so until sauce is slightly thickened.

DIPPIN' COCK

Serves 6

When you try this dish, you'll think you've converted your kitchen into a 4-star Chinese restaurant. Although it would traditionally be made with a young, spring chicken, the long steaming makes the cock meat fall off the bone and the rich stock at the bottom of the pot is reserved and used to flavor and fortify other recipes such as soups and rice dishes.

Ingredients:

> 1 whole cock
>
> 1 Tbs coarse sea salt

DIPPIN' SAUCE

Ingredients:

> 2 Tbs peanut oil or unhydrogenated lard
>
> 2 tsp toasted sesame oil
>
> 5 Tbs scallions, finely chopped
>
> 1 inch ginger, finely grated
>
> 1 tsp sugar or raw honey
>
> 3 Tbs fermented soy sauce
>
> ¼ tsp sea salt

Sprinkle salt inside and on the outer surface of cock. Place a heat-proof plate or bowl in the pasta insert of a large pasta pot. Pour enough water in pasta pot to reach just below the pasta insert. Place salted cock on plate, breast side down, and assemble the pot, covering with lid. Steam for 2 hours. About 15 minutes before serving, gently heat oils together in a small pan. Put remaining sauce ingredients in a small bowl or ramekin. When wisps of smoke begin to appear above the warm oils, pour over rest of sauce ingredients. Stand back as this may spatter slightly. Lift cock from pasta pot and place on serving platter. Serve with dipping sauce on the side or poured over meat and brown rice. The deliciously rich stock in the bottom of the pasta pot may also be served as additional flavoring for the rice or used in other recipes, such as the soup variation below.

VARIATION:

Ingredients:

Leftover cock meat from Dippin' Cock recipe

1 quart of rich stock left over from Dippin' Cock recipe

2 bunches dried mung bean or cellophane noodles

Dried shiitake mushrooms, soaked in cool water to cover for 30 minutes

Assortment of vegetables such as string bean, carrots, potatoes, spinach, broccoli, etc

Kimchee (optional)

Leftover dippin' sauce   from Dippin' Cock recipe

Simmer stock in 2-3 quart pot. Slice hard vegetables such as potatoes and carrots thin and add to stock. Cook for 5 minutes. Lift mushrooms from soaking water being careful allow any grit to sink to the bottom of water. Slice caps thinly. Add mushrooms, noodles, softer vegetables and most of mushroom water (remembering to not add grit that sank to the bottom). Cook 3 minutes longer or until desired color and texture is reached. If desired, put 2 tablespoons of kimchee at the bottom of each bowl. Pour soup into bowls. Dippin' sauce can be poured on top of each serving as a condiment.

MOROCCAN STEAMED COCK

Serves 6

Ingredients:

1 whole cock

2 big pinches of saffron, rubbed

1 inch piece of fresh ginger, grated

2 cloves garlic, minced fine

1/4 cup butter

1 Tbs coarse sea salt

Ground cumin and sea salt to serve

Mix saffron, ginger, garlic and butter together. Rub over the cock's skin. Sprinkle with course salt. Place a heat-proof plate or bowl in the pasta insert of a large pasta pot. Pour enough water in pasta pot to reach just below the pasta insert. Place seasoned cock on plate, breast side down, and assemble the pot, covering with lid. Steam for 2 hours or until cock is cooked through and tender. Serve immediately with cumin and salt for dipping.

MOROCCAN COCK STEW WITH VEGETABLES

Serves 8

In addition to lamb, Moroccan cuisine is filled with savory chicken stews. While I have not found any recipes that specifically call for cock, this recipe is inspired by my large collection of international cookbooks.

Ingredients:

1 cock, quartered

4 large onions, chopped into large pieces

4 cloves garlic, crushed

1 cup dried chickpeas, soaked overnight

2 big pinches of saffron, rubbed

1 inch fresh ginger, peeled

1 4-inch stick of cinnamon

1 cup butter

3 quarts water

1 1/2 lbs winter squash such as pumpkin, butternut or delicata squash, baked or steamed to soften skin, then peeled and seeded

1 lb carrots, peeled and sliced

1 Tbs sea salt

Drain chickpeas, rinse and place in a pot with one quart of fresh water to cover. Cook covered over medium heat for one hour or until tender. Meanwhile, in a large pot, place meat, onions, garlic, ginger, saffron, cinnamon stick, salt, half cup of the butter and the remaining water. Simmer for one hour. Next, add carrots to the broth and cook until tender. Then add squash and cook for another 30 minutes. Serve hot with couscous or rice.

COCK ALLA CACCIATORA

Serves 6

Ingredients:

1 cock, cut into eight pieces

2 Tbs extra virgin olive oil

2 onions, finely chopped

1 sprig rosemary

1 large red tomato, thickly sliced

1 cloves of garlic, crushed

1/4 cup white wine vinegar

2 cups dry white wine

Sea salt to taste

Heat a large frying pan, then add olive oil. Sauté meat until browned on all sides. Add garlic cloves and vinegar. Allow vinegar to evaporate. Remove meat to a plate. Next add finely chopped onions and rosemary to pan. When onion becomes golden in color, return meat to the pan along with tomato, wine and salt. Cover and cook for 90 minutes over low heat. Serve hot over polenta (made with cock stock instead of water), a slice of crusty bread or buttered flat egg noodles.

CURRIED COCK

Serves 6

Many people are turned off by the thought of curry, yet many of the same people who have told me that they hate curry have eaten it in my home and enjoyed it immensely only to learn later that they were eating curry. I believe one reason why they enjoy my version is because I actually fry the curry before adding the main ingredients. This intensifies the flavor of the spice, which would otherwise leave an insipid "raw" finish on the tongue.

Ingredients:

1 cock, cut into 8 pieces or meat reserved from making stock

2 Tbs coconut oil, lard or chicken fat

1 large onion, chopped

1 clove of garlic, minced

1 tomato, seeded and chopped

1 cup or more cock stock

2 Tbs curry powder

1 small piece scotch bonnet pepper, seeded and chopped to taste

1 inch fresh ginger, grated

1 tsp dried thyme

salt to taste

Heat oil over medium heat in large sauté pan. Add chopped onion. Cook 3 minutes until soft. Add garlic, thyme and curry powder. Continue to cook 2 minutes stirring not to burn garlic or curry. Add cock pieces, browning on all sides. Add tomato, scotch bonnet, ginger and stock to barely cover meat in pan. Cover pan with lid and cook for 1 – 1 ½ hours or until meat is tender. If using reserved cock meat, then add only 1 cup stock to moisten and skip long stewing time. Allow gravy to thicken by continuing to cook with lid off the pan several minutes. Add salt to taste. Serve hot with brown rice or steamed potatoes. Serves 4-6.

COCK-O'S

Serves 8-10

It always disturbs me when fast foods like tacos get a bad rap for being unhealthy simply because some fast food restaurants have chosen to serve low quality ingredients. This recipe for cock-o's proves that even fast food can be healthy and satisfying.

Ingredients:

Cock meat reserved from making stock

Taco shells (hard or soft)

Fixin's such as lettuce, tomato, guacamole, grated raw milk cheese, refried beans, salsa, chopped raw onion and sour cream

Hot sauce

Line taco shell with one of your stickier fixin's like refried beans or raw milk cheese. Add generous helping of cock meat. Top with whatever other fixin's you want. Enjoy.

REFRIED BEANS

Ingredients:

1 cup dried pinto beans

filtered water

large pinch baking soda

1 large onion, chopped finely

4-8 Tbs unhydrogenated lard

1 bay leaf

sea salt to taste

Soak beans in 2 cups filtered water with a large pinch of baking soda for 8 hours or overnight. The next day drain beans well, rinse, and drain again. Place beans in a pot with 1 quart filtered water. Bring water to the boil, then reduce to simmer. Cook about 40 minutes or until tender. Meanwhile, in a large sauté pan, melt 4 tablespoons of lard. Add onion and cook gently until onion is completely wilted and translucent. Drain beans, reserving cooking water. Add beans to onions and mash well with a potato masher. Add bay leaf, salt to taste and a cup of the cooking water. Continue to cook over low heat, stirring constantly. Add rest of lard one tablespoon at a time and stir to incorporate. Serve hot or cold.

GUACAMOLE

Ingredients:

2 ripe avocados

Juice of one lime

½ small onion, finely chopped

1 tomatillo, finely chopped (optional)

2 Tbs fresh cilantro (Chinese coriander), finely chopped

Serrano chili to taste

Cut avocados in half. Remove pits, reserving one. Scoop flesh from avocados with a spoon, then mash in a bowl with the back of a fork. Add lime juice to prevent browning. Add rest of ingredients. Place pit in middle to further retard browning. Serve cold.

COCK WITH PRUNES

Serves 6

Prunes are a fruit that is often overlooked, but so very delicious when cooked with meats. If possible, seek out *Pruneaux d'Agen*, French prunes which are widely accepted to be the best in the world.

Ingredients:

1 cock, cut into 8 serving pieces

1/2 cup dried pitted prunes

1/4 cup butter

1 large onion, finely chopped

1 clove garlic, chopped

3 medium tomatoes chopped

1 cup stock

1/2 cup dry sherry

Sea salt to taste

Soak prunes in a bowl of hot water to soften. Set aside. Meanwhile, melt butter in a large frying pan. Cook meat to brown on all sides. Add onion and garlic. When onion is golden, add tomatoes. Drain prunes and chop. Add to meat mixture. Season with salt, cover and cook over low heat for 1 hour or until meat is tender. Five to 10 minutes before serving, add sherry. Adjust seasoning and serve.

DRUNKEN COCK

Serves 6

Ingredients:

   1 cock, cut into 8 serving pieces

   2 Tbs extra virgin olive oil or unhydrogenated lard

   2 Tbs butter

   1/4 lb ham, chopped

   1 cup seedless raisins

   1/8 tsp each: ground cloves, cinnamon, cumin and
   coriander seed

   2 cloves garlic, chopped

   2 cups dry white wine

   1/2 cup toasted, slivered almonds

   1/2 cup pitted green olives

   1 Tbs capers, drained and rinsed

   Sea salt to taste

Heat olive oil and butter in a large flameproof pan with tight fitting
lid. Add meat and cook on all sides until golden. Add ham, raisins,
spices, garlic and wine. Cover and cook for 1 1/2 hours or until

tender. Remove cover and add remaining ingredients. Cook for 5 minutes uncovered. Adjust seasonings and serve.

COCK POT ROAST

Serves 6

Ingredients:

1 whole cock

1/2 lb butter, softened

1 cup filtered water

1 bunch parsley, chopped

1/2 tsp sea salt

Sea salt to taste

Rub together half the butter, parsley and salt. Stuff this mixture inside the bird. Melt butter in a Dutch oven and brown the meat on all sides. Add water to prevent scorching and add moisture to ensure the meat is not tough. Sprinkle a bit more salt over the cock. Cover pot and cook over low heat for 3 hours or until meat is tender. Remove cock to a warm platter. Pour a few tablespoons of water into the bottom of the pot to loosen any hardened bits. Serve this sauce over the cock to serve.

DESSERTS

COCK PUDDING

Serves 12

I first learned of this famous Turkish chicken dessert on my first trip to Turkey back in the mid 1990s. The concept of using meat in a dessert sounds crazy to Americans, but it is quite tasty. You can easily use the meat reserved from making cock stock, but because this is not a savory dish, you will likely want to make it without any seasonings whatsoever. That said, after removing the meat needed for this dish, you can add all the savory seasonings you want to the remaining meat and broth and continue as usual. Alternately, cut away the breast meat and continue as noted below.

Ingredients:

Breast meat of one cock

2 quarts whole milk (not ultra-pasteurized)

1 1/2 cups sugar

1 1/3 cups rice flour

Simmer meat in a pot of water until meat is tender. Drain and shred the meat into fine hairs by rubbing it between the palms of your hands (consider saving the cooking water to use in soups or sauces or for making dishes like risotto). Soak the "hairs" in a cup of water for 2 minutes then squeeze to remove excess water. Set aside.

Put sugar and rice flour in a heavy-bottomed pot. With pot over medium heat, slowly pour in cold milk, stirring constantly. Allow mixture to come to a boil for 10 minutes allowing it to thicken. Stir in meat and allow to continue to boil. Pour into dessert bowls and allow to set. Sprinkle the top of each pudding with cinnamon. Serve lukewarm or cold.

BASICS

BAKING POWDER

I haven't bought baking powder in over 15 years. It's so simple and inexpensive to make yourself, there's no reason not to.

Ingredients:

4 Tbs arrowroot starch

4 Tbs cream of tartar

2 Tbs baking soda

Mix all ingredients together. Store in a tightly closed jar.

BASIC PIE CRUST
(ALL WHITE FLOUR)

Makes 2 10-inch pie crusts

When rolling out this dough, the process should go rather quickly, but if you're new to pie making, you may want to refrigerate the second half of the butter mixture while working on the first to ensure a flaky final dough.

Ingredients:

2 cups unbleached white flour

¼ tsp fine sea salt

2 cups cold butter or 1 cup cold butter and 1 cup non-hydrogenated lard

½ C ice water

Place flour in a mixing bowl with salt. Cut fat into small pieces and add to flour. Using tips of fingers, break up fat into even smaller pieces until mixture resembles a coarse meal. Gradually add ice water, mixing all the time with fingers or a fork. Stop adding water when mixture holds together and is still pliable, but not sticky. Depending on humidity, you may need more or less water. Gather dough into a ball, cover well with plastic wrap and refrigerate for at least 30 minutes and up to 24 hours.

When ready to bake, remove dough from refrigerator and cut into two equal pieces. Reshape each piece into a disk. Take one disk, sprinkle with flour on both sides and place on a square piece of wax paper. Cover top with another equal sized piece of wax paper.

Using a rolling pin, roll out dough to an 11" circle. Repeat process with the other disk. Use as described in recipes.

BASIC PIE CRUST
(WITH WHOLE WHEAT)

Makes 2 10-inch pie crusts

This crust uses some whole wheat for those seeking some extra nutrition and yields a slightly crisper crust than the all white flour version. When rolling out this dough, the process should go rather quickly, but if you're new to pie making, you may want to refrigerate the second half of the butter mixture while working on the first to ensure a flaky final dough.

Ingredients:

> 1 ½ cup whole-wheat flour
>
> 1/2 cup water
>
> juice of ½ lemon or 2 Tbs yogurt
>
> 1 cup unbleached white flour, plus more for dusting
>
> ¼ tsp salt
>
> 1 cup chilled butter (or ½ cup butter and ½ cup unhydrogenated lard)

In a bowl, mix whole-wheat flour with water and lemon juice or yogurt to make a soft, pliable dough that holds together, but is not dry. Cover with a plate and let rest at room temperature for 7-24 hours.

When ready to proceed, mix unbleached flour and salt in a separate bowl. Cut in butter, then break it up into the flour with your cool fingertips until the butter is in pea-sized, well-coated pieces.

Divide whole-wheat dough into two pieces. On a floured wooden board, roll one piece of dough into a paper-sized rectangle. Place half of the floured butter into the center of the rectangle, then fold whole-wheat dough over it in thirds, like a letter. Roll this out with a rolling pin so as to lengthen the short side, making a square. If butter squeezes out the sides, fold buttery ends in towards the center again like a letter and roll out, making sure to dust the board, rolling pin and dough with flour as necessary.

Dough can now be rolled thin, laid in a pie plate and trimmed down to size or you can round out the corners by folding the edges down towards center in several places into an octagonal shape and rolling out into a circle. Repeat with second piece of whole-wheat dough and remaining floured butter. Use as described in recipes.

BOUQUET GARNI

Bouquet garni is an herbal packet standard in many French-inspired recipes. The packet, or bouquet, is comprised of herbs tied together with kitchen string so that it can be easily removed from the final dish. In some cases, it is tied together with the thyme, which has a strong, woody yet flexible stem that stands up to long cooking. The ingredients may vary, but below is a fairly universal version.

Ingredients:

4 sprigs of thyme

1 bay leaf

4 or 5 sprigs of parsley

1/2 stick of celery

Tie all ingredients together in a small piece of muslin or tie them together with a long sprig of thyme. Use in soups and stews. Fish out the herbs before serving.

SCOTTISH BOUQUET

Use this bouquet in Cock-a-Leekie. Remove from pot before serving.

Ingredients:

1 clove

1 sprig of parsley

6 peppercorns

Tie all in a muslin sack.

MAYONNAISE

I learned to make mayonnaise while living in Spain. I often buy mayonnaise these days, but when time allows, I like to make this one. The key to making a great mayonnaise is to beat the yolks quickly while adding the oil very, very slowly at first. If you add the oil too quickly, the mayonnaise will break, leaving you with and egg mixture that has oil floating on top.

Ingredients:

    2 egg yolks

    2 cups light-flavored extra virgin olive oil such as French olive oil

    2 Tbs freshly squeezed lemon juice

    Pinch of salt

Place egg yolks, 1/2 tablespoon of the lemon juice and salt in a one-quart measuring cup. Blend thoroughly with whisk or stick blender. While blending, begin drizzling olive oil into egg yolk mixture one drop at a time. As the mixture begins to thicken, you can begin adding oil in a stream. Beat in remaining lemon juice a little at a time. Use on sandwiches, coquettes, meats, seafood or fries.

PESTO SAUCE

Ingredients:

30 large, fresh basil washed and dried with a towel

1 clove garlic

Pinch of salt

Extra virgin olive oil

2 Tbs of finely grated hard, salty cheese such as Parmagiano Reggiano, romano or ricotta salata (crumbled)

2 Tbs pine nuts (if unavailable, almonds or even sunflower seeds work well too)

Toast nuts in a sauce pan, crush and reserve. In the bowl of a food processor, place basil along with the salt and garlic. Make sure the garlic where it is less likely to get stuck in large chunks. Start motor of processor, then begin to drizzle in olive oil. Continue adding oil until a thick cream is achieved. Turn out sauce into a bowl. Fold in cheese and nuts. Use on pasta, pizza, breads or meats.

APPENDIX

MEASUREMENTS & EQUIVALENTS

a dash = 8 drops (liquid) ≈ ⅛ teaspoon (slightly less)

1 tsp = 1 teaspoon = 60 drops

3 tsp = 3 teaspoons = 1 tablespoon = ½ fluid ounce

½ T = ½ tablespoon = 1½ teaspoons

2 T = 2 tablespoons (liquid) = 1 fluid ounce = ⅛ cup

3 T = 3 tablespoons = 1 ½ fluid ounces = 1 jigger

4 T = 4 tablespoons = ¼ cup

⅛ C = ⅛ cup = 2 tablespoons

⅙ C = ⅙ cup = 2 tablespoons + 2 teaspoons

⅓ C = ⅓ cup = 5 tablespoons + 1 teaspoon

1 C = 1 cup = ½ pint = 8 fluid ounces

2 C = 2 cups = 1 pint = 16 fluid ounces

4 C = 4 cups = 1 quart = 2 pints = 32 fluid ounces

4 quarts = 1 gallon

1 peck = 8 quarts = 2 gallons

1 bushel = 4 pecks

RESOURCES

Bock, Linda, *State Doesn't Know if Listeriosis Outbreak is Over*, News Telegram, January 2008.

Brownstein, David, *Salt Your Way to Health*, Medical Alternative Press, 2006.

Byrnes, Stephen, *Diet & Heart Disease: It's NOT What You Think...*, Whitman Publications, 2001.

Enig, Mary, *Know Your Fats: The Complete Primer for Understanding the Nutrition of Fats, Oils, and Cholesterol*, Bethesda Press, 2000.

Enig, Mary and Sally Fallon, *Nourishing Traditions: The Cookbook that Challenges Politically Correct Nutrition and the Diet Dictocrats*, Hudson Street Press, 1995.

Fleming, D.W., S.L. Cochi, et al., *Pasteurized Milk as a Vehicle of Infection in an Outbreak of Listeriosis*, The New England Journal of Medicine, Volume 312:404-407, February 14, 1985.

Lu, Henry C., *Chinese Natural Cures: Traditional Methods for Remedies and Preventions*, Black Dog & Leventhal Publishers, Inc., 1994.

Pizzorno, Joseph E. and Michael T. Murray, *Textbook of Natural Medicine*, Churchill Livingstone, 2000.

Pritchford, Paul, *Healing with Whole Foods: Oriental Traditions and Modern Traditions*, North Atlantic Books, 1993.

Monastyrsky, Konstantin, *Fiber Menace: The Truth About the Leading Role of Fiber in Diet Failure, Constipation, Hemorrhoids, Irritable Bowel Syndrome, Ulcerative Colitis, Crohn's Disease, and Colon Cancer*, Ageless Press, 2005.

Ryan, C.A., M.K. Nickels et al., *Massive Outbreak of Antimicrobial-Resistant Salmonellosis Traced to Pasteurized Milk,*

The Journal of the American Medical Association, Vol. 258 No. 22, December 11, 1987.

Vonderplanitz, Aajonus, *We Want to Live*, Carnelian Bay Castle Press, LLC, 1997.

Whitney, E.N. and S.R. Rolfes, *Understanding Nutrition*, Ninth Edition, Wadsworth Group, 2002.

Williams, David G., *Conquering Arthritis Through Natural Methods*, Mountain Home Publishing, 1994.

OTHER BOOKS YOU MIGHT ENJOY

Nourishing Traditions by Sally Fallon Morell and Dr. Mary Enig

Kitchen Confidential by Anthony Bourdain

LIKE THE BOOK?

I hope you enjoyed reading this book as much as I enjoyed writing it. If you did, I'd really appreciate a quick review on the Amazon.com website (http://nutritionheretic.com/50Ways).

Of course, I'm always looking to improve as well. So if you think there is something that I can do better for my next book or have any ideas for new topics you'd like to see, please reach out to me on Facebook (http://www.facebook.com/TheNutritionHeretic) and let me know.

SPECIAL GIFTS FOR YOU!

Want a sneak peek at some outrageously delicious recipes from my new book, *Honeylingus: 50 Healthy Honey Recipes that Will Leave You Begging for More*? Looking for more information on what's safe and healthy to eat? Want *real* answers to your health questions?

Grab all these and more by going to http://honeyling.us to claim your FREE gifts today!

ABOUT THE AUTHOR

Adrienne Hew has been called "the Nutrition Heretic" and "the Pope of Health" because of the unique sense of levelheadedness she brings to discussions on nutrition. Both Dietetic Associations and politically correct, so-called alternative health advocates often have difficulty reconciling their beliefs with the truth contained in her observations and experiences.

Ms. Hew began her holistic health journey after suffering innumerable health problems and near death experiences while following the American Dietetics Association's dietary recommendations. Born into a multicultural family that had thrived on a very different diet, she set on a quest to learn the dietary commonalities amongst all healthy societies. Her fluency in three languages has enabled her to uncover many long forgotten food traditions throughout the world.

Receiving a certificate in Chinese dietetics in 2002 and her degree as a Certified Nutritionist in 2004, she has helped many clients and workshop attendees to decode their own health dilemmas by understanding the inconsistencies in conventional nutritional dogma. As a cook, her recipes have been popular with everyone from celebrated chefs to picky 4 year olds and adults who "don't eat that". She currently resides in Hawaii with her husband and two children.

She can be found online at http://www.nutritionheretic.com as well as on her Facebook fan page (http://www.facebook.com/TheNutritionHeretic) and on Twitter (http://twitter.com/NutriHeretic).

Made in the USA
Columbia, SC
21 November 2017